BAINTE DEN STOC

WITHDRAWN FROM DLR LIBRARIES STOCK

bradshaw books
Tigh Filí, Civic Trust House, Pope's Quay, Cork
www.eurochild.net

© The Authors 2011
ISBN: 978-1-905374-23-6

This book is sold subject to the condition that it will not, by way of trade or otherwise, be lent, resold, hired out or otherwise circulated without the publisher's prior consent in any form of binding or cover other than that in which it is published and without a similar condition being imposed on the subsequent purchaser.

Cover artwork by Fanni Toszegi
Cover design by Aisling Lyons
Book design by panorama@indigo.ie
Printed by Gemini

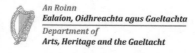

Eurochild

Edited by

Aoileann Lyons

bradshaw books
Cork, Ireland

Letter from the European Commission for Education, Culture, Multilingualism & Youth

I am truly delighted to hear of the ongoing success of Eurochild. The dedicated effort of Tigh Filí to enhance the cultural capacities of children from different cultures by bringing them together through art and poetry is remarkable and deserves full support.

Actions such as the Eurochild Anthology of Children's Artwork and Poetry greatly enrich European culture and showcase both the talent of European children and the multicultural, multilingual world in which we all live. I am especially impressed by the enthusiasm shown for the scheme throughout Europe and the 1,000s of young artists and poets involved bear testament to the superb work and commitment of Tigh Filí.

It is also extremely commendable that the project has become a member of Eurochild.org. [...] this new partnership demonstrates the capacity for culture to develop and expand along new and interesting lines in Europe.

With 2011 being designated as the European Union's Year of Volunteering, I particularly welcome the extensive use the Eurochild project makes of volunteers and of how it relies on the goodwill of individuals.

I trust that the excellent work of Tigh Filí in fostering dialogue, integration and cultural literacy between children from all over Europe through the Eurochild programme will long continue. This will certainly help promote those values that are at the very heart of the European integration process.

Philippe Brunet
Chef de Cabinet European Commission for Education, Culture, Multilingualism and Youth

Foreword by the Minister for Foreign Affairs and Trade

I feel honoured to have been invited to write an introduction to this wonderful Eurochild Anthology of Poetry and Art.

I would like to salute the artists and authors who have contributed to this year's edition. Their work is vibrant and original and I was particularly struck by the sense of yearning for peace, security and social justice that pervades many of the verses and images. It is a real source of hope for the future that a new generation of Europeans shares and champions these values.

I would also like to congratulate the Eurochild project on its continuing success in bringing together young poets and artists from all corners of Europe. Readers of this anthology will draw great inspiration from their creativity.

I hope that the project will be a springboard and inspiration for these young people and that they will continue to make their voices heard. In doing so, they will shape and enrich the lives of those around them.

Eamon Gilmore T.D.
Tánaiste and Minister for Foreign Affairs and Trade

What our friends say...

Ever since I got a copy, I have kept the last Eurochild Anthology on my desk. The reason is simple. If I need a bit of cheering up, or sometimes a bit of inspiration, I know I can open it at random and read a poem that lightens my mood. And I love the artwork – it's simple, direct, and really expressive. There's a huge amount of truth in the book and in the individual pieces.

So I often quote these pieces in speeches, or rely on them to illustrate points I want to make. If I want to talk about hope or despair, courage or struggle, loneliness or friendship, someone young has written something from their own heart and I can find it in the Anthology. But pictures of landscapes and ghosts, houses and trees, and perhaps above all pictures of the people we love (from Mum and Dad to imaginary friends) have the capacity to inspire new ideas too.

You can't read the Anthology without being full of admiration and respect for the talent and work of the young people involved. And you can't read it either without enjoying the sheer fun of it.

I can't wait for the 2011 edition!

Fergus Finlay
CEO Barnardos Ireland

The Eurochild Anthology is a very special and unique publication. Published in Cork, it is a vehicle which allows children not only to explore and celebrate their literary and artistic skills but also to share their work with children and school communities from all over Europe. This year's publication contains contributions from over twenty countries and it is wonderful to see that more countries have joined the project this year.

As in previous years, a large number of children from schools involved in the Modern Languages in Primary Schools Initiative are represented in the anthology. While it is wonderful to see and read work from children around Europe in their own mother tongues, it has been especially heartening to see that so many children choose to use the modern language they are learning in primary school for their selected works.

We in the Modern Languages in Primary Schools Initiative will continue to promote the Eurochild Anthology to teachers and schools as an excellent cultural and linguistic resource and we wish it and its dedicated publishing team continued inspiration and success.

Tanya Flanagan
National Co-ordinator Modern Languages in Primary Schools Initiative

Creating a beautiful poem or artistic image is not a simple task; it is a complex creative leap into the imagination and often a reflection of the innermost thoughts of the writer or artist. We do not always associate great poetry or indeed great art with children or younger people. A glance at some of the wonderful works in this latest Eurochild anthology shows how extraordinary poetry and beautiful imagery appear just as equally from the minds of children and young people as they do from mature adults.

One of the primary aims of the Eurochild project is to develop informed active young citizens through the arts, as an effective complement to other political and social education initiatives. It is clear from reading through this collection that children do not carry the baggage that adults sometimes have. Their words and imagery are generally therefore devoid of ideology, and full of hope and wonderment at what is possible in the modern world. I believe passionately that the voices of children must be heard in a real and meaningful way. I am heartened at recent developments both at EU level and also nationally here in Ireland where the child and youth participation agenda is gradually gaining momentum to ensure real influence by young citizens in framing public policy. As the first full Irish cabinet Minister for Children and Youth Affairs, I will work to ensure that this work is continued and extended in the coming years.

In this wonderful anthology we see how the thoughts and aspirations of children reflected through art and poetry open our minds to a whole new world of possibilities for all of us in which creative expression can help to shed light on the issues most important to children and younger people. Each of the contributions has something meaningful to say and, as adults, we must ensure we learn uniquely from them. In many cases children can draw our attention to issues that we may not even have considered or thought about.

Eurochild allows us to hear from children all over the world and also this year, as last, from older children and teenagers. I applaud all those involved in this important project, now in its 16th year, and look forward to even more original and groundbreaking work in the future.

Frances Fitzgerald TD.
Minister for Children & Youth Affairs

POETRY

euroteen

ARTWORK

Сакам да бидам…
(I Want To Be…)

Сакам да копаат
Монети стар со векови
Сакам да копа длабоко во калапот
Сакам да најдам хиероглифи
За да ја прочитате,
Сакам да бидам археолог

Сакам да се подготви мостови и згради,
Сакам да им помогне на луѓето да ги направи,
Ќе бидат задолжени за проектите целосна листа,
Сакам да бидам археолог

Сакам да патувам
До Сатурн, Венера и Плутон,
Јас дури и би можело да стане простор Султан
Сакам да работам без пауза,
Сакам да бидам астронаут

Всушност, јас сум се уште не се сигурни,
Што сакам да бидам,
Кога ќе добијам малку постара
Јас ќе видиме.

Сакам да бидам… *by* Anastasija Petlichkovska, OU Johan Hajnrih Pestaloci, Skopje, Macedonia
All Together Forever *by* Dorothy Hedderman, Scoil Mhuire Junior School, Cork

1

عائدون
(Returning)

للبيوت و السهر   عائدون للديار
للتراث و السمر   عائدون للأشعار
للظلال و الثمر   عائدون للشجر
تحت أنوار القمر   عائدون للكروم
للمزارع و النهر   عائدون للحقول
نسمع تغريد الكنر   عائدون للمروج
سوف نردد عائدون

Le Rondini
(Swallows)

Le rondini si preparano a viaggiare
Come turisti si sanno a organizzare
Dove andranno non lo sanno
Ma di certo un giorno torneranno
Quando torneranno
La primavera profumata
Porteranno.

Returning *by Roba Ayed Zohod, Nuseirat Elementary Girls B, Nuseirat Camp, Gaza*
2 Le Rondini *by Aurora del Signore, Scuola Primaria dell'Istituto Comprensivo 'P. Serafini – L. di Stefano', Sulmona, Italy*
Storks *by Sofiya Budyanskaya, Alexandrovskaya Gymnasia, Sumy, Ukraine*

El Color
(Colour)

El amarillo
Es un color
Como tu colorido
Corazón rojo
Como tu amor

Cuando huelo tu olor
Me siento
Con el hermoso olor
De tu corazón

El rojizo
Es una mezcla
De tu colorido
Y hermoso corazón

Cuando veo tu hermoso rostro
Estoy encantado
De enamorarme de vos.

Rainbow

Some people are blue
Or yellow or orange
Or red or purple
But I am different
I am a rainbow.

El Color by Florencio Morón, Sunflower School, Buenos Aires, Argentina
Rainbow by Holly O'Connell, GS an Ghoirt Álainn, Cork

Im Kaufhaus Ohne Was im Magen
(In the Supermarket With Nothing in my Tum)

Mit leerem Magen kaufen,
das würd' ich eher nicht,
denn darüber erzähl ich dir
jetzt folgende Geschicht'

Im Kaufhaus wollt' Fred eigentlich,
nur ein Bisschen sehen,
mal hier, mal da,
mal rings herum,
und dann schon wieder gehen.
Kaum kommt er in den Laden rein,
da fällt ihm alles wieder ein

Dort drüben ist das Fleisch,
und da viel Süßigkeit,
da macht sich in sein' Blicken
die Apfelsine breit.
Daneben sind noch Beeren,
dort drüben ist noch Speck,
so geht es immer weiter,
und um die nächste Eck'

Nachher geht er zur Kasse
So teuer? Ach so'n Scheiß!
Sein Rucksack schwer,
das Portmo' leer,
und das ist jetzt sein Preis.

4 Im Kaufhaus Ohne Was im Magen *by Marei Mießler, Musikschule der Hansestadt Wismar, Germany*
Shopping Hungry *by Marei Mießler, Musikschule der Hansestadt Wismar, Germany*

What Would Happen If?

What would happen if school were fun
What would happen if my homework was done
What would happen if my friends were torn
What would happen if I wasn't born?

Would anyone feel like something was missing?
Or would they always be too busy?

What Would Happen If? by Niamh Quinn, Scoil Mhuire Gan Smál, Ballymote, Co. Sligo
The Happy Ants by Petra Vinkler, Belvárosi Óvoda és Általános Iskola, Kecskemét, Hungary

The Jumping Game

We jump the rope
We jump in line
We jump up high
We jump in time
We jump for luck
We jump again
We jump along
The jumping game

We jump in ones
We jump in twos
We jump the lights
We jump the queues
We jump for joy
We jump again
We jump along
The jumping game

We jump and fall
We jump and learn
We jump and twist
We jump and turn
We jump for kicks
We jump again
We jump along
The jumping game

We jump for gold
We jump for free
We jump from A
We jump to B
We jump for fun
We jump again
We jump along
The jumping game.

6 The Jumping Game *by* Cathy Ní Luinneacháin, Scoil Chaitlín Naofa, Tralee, Co. Kerry
We Have a Right to Leisure *by* Sergei Novikov, Smorgon Educational Centre for Children and Youth, Belarus

In the Park

Our park is cool
I play there after school
I swing on the swings
Up ever so high
See me go high
See me go low
See me go fast
Faster then slow
The slides are fun
I go up there after
I climb up the rocks
And get to the top
And then I slide down
With a jump and a hop.

In the Park *by* Laura Kennedy, Scoil Mhuire NS, Schull, Co. Cork

Chi Ama la Natura *by* Nicole Olivero, Scuola Primaria dell'Istituto Comprensivo 'P. Serafini – L. di Stefano', Sulmona, Italy

A Christmas Star

Oh Christmas star
As sparkling as the moonlight
It's a shiny diamond
And twinkling through the sky

It's as bright as the glowing light
As attractive as a lovely lamb
Like a special, unique person
A silver guiding star

It's a marvellous giant
With five pointed corners
A saviour star
There to guide me!

Zima
(Winter)

Všude bílá peřina
takhle zima začíná
Děti se honí v závěji
pak u kamen se zahřejí
Jen zvířátka jsou hladová
proč je zima taková?

A Christmas Star *by* Luca Falzon, Stella Maris College, Ġzira, Malta
Zima *by* Zuzana Vyskočilová, Gymnázium Jiřího Ortena, Kutná Hora, Czech Republic

Tree

Lots of words,
Left unsaid
Before

The boards in the attic,
So old and creaky
Tell stories
Of the big oak tree
Planted near the river

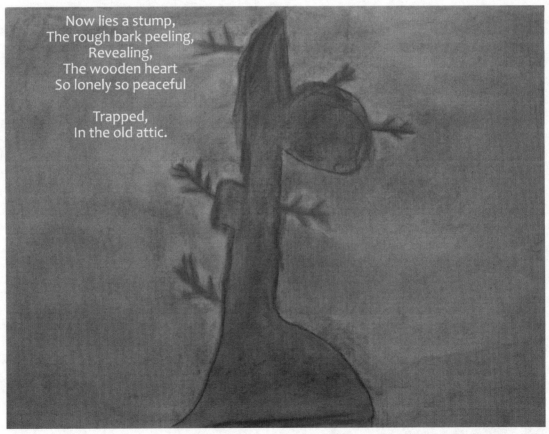

Now lies a stump,
The rough bark peeling,
Revealing,
The wooden heart
So lonely so peaceful

Trapped,
In the old attic.

Tree *by* Foster Piotrow, Jackson Grammar School, New Hampshire, USA
Cactus Tree *by* Jack Laffey, Lettergesh NS, Co. Galway

Home

I've never taken time alone
To have a look around

My cosy, comfortable bed
The sofa where I watch TV
I never realised it's so me
And the chair where I write this poem
Not to mention when I read a book
I never took the time to look
Out the window and just stare
At the wonderful garden sitting there

The comfort of my lovely house
It's the only home for me.

Home *by* Cian Donohoe, Ballyleague NS, Co. Roscommon
Home (drawing) *by* Rachel Holland, St Patrick's GNS, Cork

Patriotism

على أرض بلادي يحلو السهر	تحت ضوء القمر
العصافير كأنها رحيق و عبير	كنت أستيقظ على صوت
كأنها تتحدث معي{أحلى العبر }	كنت أشم رائحة الأزهار
أهال البيوت و الشجر	ذات يوم سمعت صوت انفجار
الناس منه و اذعر	رأيت محتلاً يعدو فخاف
لم يرحم حتى الصغر	قتل الرجال و الشيوخ
جدي في دربي هي الصبر	سأخبئ مفتاح الدار لأن وصية

Patriotism *by Roba Ayed Zohod, Nuseirat Elementary Girls B, Nuseirat Camp, Gaza*
Upside Down World *by Andrea Faherty, Lettergesh NS, Co. Galway* **11**

A Letter to Johnny

Dear Johnny,

Have you met dear Babbs above?
I'm sure she's there by now
Tell her she's part of my life
And nothing's right in Mullinaghta
Without her.

Ha Majd Felnőtt Leszel
(When You Are an Adult)

Hófehérke törpéivel
Hamupipőke hintóján
Jusson mindig eszedbe
Ez csak álomvilág

Nem igaz, csak képzeled,
S ha nagy leszel, elfeleded,
régen Hogy hittél régen a csodákban,
Tündéreknek hadában

Elfeleded a sok szépet:
A babát meg az autót,
S helyette majd jön a TV,
meg a gép és a telefon

Észre sem veszed, hogy felnőttél,
S nem gondolsz a jövődre
Nem gondolsz a múltra sem,
csak a jelenre.

12 A Letter to Johnny by Mary Rogers, St Columba's NS, Dring, Co. Longford
Ha Majd Felnőtt Leszel by Fanni Ildikó Bacsur, Székács József Evangélikus Óvoda, Általános Iskola és Gimnázium, Orosháza, Hungary
Mother and Daughter by Alma Shehu, Shkolla Kongresi i Lushnjës, Tirana, Albania

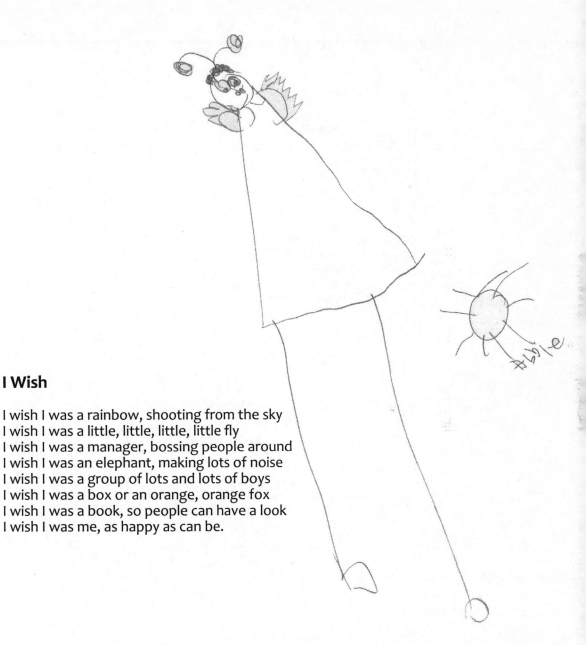

I Wish

I wish I was a rainbow, shooting from the sky
I wish I was a little, little, little, little fly
I wish I was a manager, bossing people around
I wish I was an elephant, making lots of noise
I wish I was a group of lots and lots of boys
I wish I was a box or an orange, orange fox
I wish I was a book, so people can have a look
I wish I was me, as happy as can be.

I Wish *by* Teniola Olaleye, Grianach House School, Galway
Hi To You! *by* Abbie Warren, St Patrick's GNS, Cork

Harvest Time

Here are the apples
Here the pears
Crusty bread
And cream éclairs
Potatoes and onions
Barley and rye
Honey in pots
And rhubarb pie
Berries and cherries
And bales of hay
Thanks be for the harvest
God gave us today.

Milé Jaro
(Sweet Spring)

To mé milé Jaro
zimu už přepralo
Vypučely sněženky
fialky i bledulky

Pomlázka sviští
a dívky piští
Venku je teplo a hezky
asi si vezmu ty svoje kecky.

14 Harvest Time by Romily Maguire, Scoil Mhuire Junior School, Cork
Milé Jaro by Kristián Kislinger, Gymnázium Jiřího Ortena, Kutná Hora, Czech Republic

Winter

Winter is the children's season
Snow and ice are the reason
Making snowballs, having fights
Staying outside until it's night
Making snowmen tall and fat
On its head is Daddy's hat
Sliding down the icy roads
Falling over, laughing loads
All grown ups, they hate the snow
They wish that it would really go
Grannies hate those snowy days
They pray and wish that it would rain.

When Angels Fall Down

When Angels fall down
They see what I've drawn
Mary and Joseph in the stable
And shepherds on their way
The Wise Men on camels
And turkeys in the oven
Children opening presents
And angels coming close
To see the birth of Jesus
Santa dashing about telling
The elves the good news
Snow upon snow and
Me making a snowman
Out in the garden.

Winter *by* Michael O'Mahony, Scoil Mhuire NS, Schull, Co. Cork
When Angels Fall Down *by* Meghan Finnan, St Mel's NS, Ardagh, Co. Longford
Snowman *by* Adam Buckle, Stella Maris College, Ġzira, Malta

15

Battles

History is fraught
With battles and war
I hope human kind
Can be better than before.

Battles *by* Jack Laffey, Lettergesh NS, Co. Galway
Heaven and Hell *by* Zoltan Orosz, Fiumei Úti Általános Iskola, Szolnok, Hungary

Yo y mi Papá
(Me and My Dad)

Un día fui a dormir
A la casa de un amigo
Cuando desperté
Estaba listo pa' llorar
Pero no era un llorar cualquiera

Se había muerto Papá
Con una amiga más
Que se llamaba Julieta
Y volvían de bailar.

My Dad

Neck nuzzling
Crossword puzzling
Nail picking
Towel flicking
Sleeps in
Eats from the tin
Loud snoring
Can be boring
Silly laughing
Aarf aarfing
Shopping getting
List forgetting
Football playing
Chore delaying
Slightly greying
Dad.

Yo y mi Papá *by* Benjamín Lahitte, Sunflower School, Buenos Aires, Argentina
My Dad *by* Peter O'Driscoll, Scoil Phádraig Naofa, Bandon, Co. Cork

An Siopa

Bíonn an siopa an-chiúin
Ach tá sé an-dheas
Tá sé fuar ann
Mar ní oibríonn aon teas

Tá na scoláirí ag teacht
Níl siad ciúin
Ach tá siad glórach
Cuireann siad racht i mo scórnach.

18 An Siopa by Michelle Nic Eoin, Scoil Mhaolchéadair, Muiríoch, Tralee, Co. Kerry
Sweet House by Balàzs Macsuga, Kesjár Csaba Általános Iskola, Budaörs, Hungary

The Wolf

Dark grey coat and magical eyes
You live in a land far away from me
Your body a temple of strength and honour
With you I feel safe
Wrongly accused of being the most vicious of all creatures
Like me, you're often misunderstood
You're my warrior most mystical
Of all God's creatures.

Gobbledygook

A random pear
Swimming through tape
Darting like a turtle
Racing bunnies
Galumphing through plum pudding
Gobbling fruit cake with flimsy teeth
Singing John Lennon
For no apparent reason
It spews its gobbledygook
At no one who is listening

The Wolf *by* Aoife Ní Mhathúna, GS Bheanntraí, Co. Cork
Gobbledygook *by* Darren Piotrow, Jackson Grammar School, New Hampshire, USA
Frog *by* Tyra Burke, Presentation Primary School, Bandon, Cork

19

My Puppy

My lovely puppy is a very playful puppy
She loves the sound 'squeak'
But hates the sounds 'bang and crash'
She loves her bed
To eat I think
She ripped it to bits
Now she has a new bed.

 My Puppy *by* Patrick O'Leary, Dyslexic Association of Ireland, Cork
Puppy *by* Muireann Vallely, GS an Ghoirt Álainn, Cork

Decorating the Christmas Tree

Decorating the Christmas tree
Fills my heart with joy
Putting on the tinsel
And the fairy lights
It's awesome to see
Those familiar lights
On again before my eyes
The hanging decorations
Swing while the tree
Just stands there
Pretty as day.

Christmas Eve Night

It was Christmas Eve night
The Christmas tree lights were on
Our stockings were up on a height
But there were no reindeer in sight
We were waiting for a glimpse
Before we went to sleep
The night seemed long
Then suddenly I saw something alight
We ran up
But Santa was on such a tight schedule
That he was already in flight.

Decorating the Christmas Tree *by* Leanne Courtney, St Dominic's NS, Kenagh, Co. Longford
Christmas Eve Night *by* Aidan Murtagh, Emper NS, Ballynacargy, Co. Westmeath

The Way the World Was Put Together

The eternal fire that warms our hearts
The flowing water that quenches our thirst
The mass of air that fills our lungs
The fertile earth that shelters life
The four elements clash together
Counteracting and equalising the world

The four elements fight an everlasting battle
Together destroying and creating at will
All four elements are creation
Just as all four can breathe death
Entwined like the colours of a rainbow
Strong and dependable through the night

And though the elements fight an ongoing battle
And though they clash and fight
It's the way the world was put together
Counteracting and equalising the world.

The Way the World Was Put Together *by* Adam Farrell, Ballyleague NS, Co. Roscommon
Mum and Me *by* Aoife Nixon, Scoil Phádraig Naofa, Rochestown, Cork

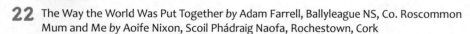

The Toy Shop

I see it there standing tall
With a big red door
And a stone-cut wall
There's a big glass window
full of toys inside
And children looking,
with their eyes open wide

I'm standing beside them
I'm looking to hold Mum's hand
Wondering what she will do
Because today is my birthday
I'm 7 years old
I really do hope
My favourite doll is not sold

Mum reaches for it on the top shelf
I can hear her say to herself
'Oh, I hope she will like it'
As she purchases it and I say my farewells
To all the other toys sitting on the shelves

Mum hands me the doll
I name her Lily Blue
I can't wait to experience
All the things we can do.

Tomás agus an Chathaoir

Bhí Tomás ina shuí i gcathaoir an rí
Tar éis cupla lá thit sé ar an urlár
Thosaigh sé ag gol ar nós babaí bhig
Tháinig a Mhamaí agus chonaic sí é

Thóg sí in airde é ón urlár
Agus duirt sí, 'Ná bí ag gol,
Imeoimid go dtí an siopa
Agus ceannóidh mé rud éigin deas duit
D'éist sé léi agus bhí gach rud ceart go leor.

The Toy Shop *by* Gigi d'Avilez, Rockboro PS, Cork
Tomás agus an Chathaoir *by* Pádraig Ó Ciobháin, Scoil Mhaolchéadair, Muiríoch, Tralee, Co. Kerry
Friends *by* Bridzeta Rainika, Ballyleague NS, Co. Roscommon

23

The First Creation

One day in heaven above
God was feeling full of love
Talking to a peaceful dove
He decided to create land to love

For seven days and nights he worked
Lightning stormed and seas lurched
'Add some land,' the Dove urged
And God did so, but the land wasn't merged

Fish and animals reigned the land
But he didn't forget the ants in the sand
God reached out with a working hand
And said, 'Here there shall be man!'

Years went by and humans achieved
How to talk and how to believe
'Let's give birth,' said Adam to Eve
Eve said yes, she had to agree

Cane and Abel came along
Singing a very happy song
Abel didn't live very long
'Coz Cane killed Abel right after the sacrifice song.

24 The First Creation *by* Dylan Odom, Stella Maris College, Ġzira, Malta
Come On, Sister! *by* Leah Reynolds, Scoil Mhuire gan Smál, Ballymote, Co. Sligo

J'Adore le Skateboard
(I Love Skateboarding)

J'adore le skate board
Je suis très rapide
Je monte sur la rampe
Et je glisse sur la pente
Je fais du free style avec mes copains
Qu'est-ce que c'est bien!

Animals *by* Eszter Hardi, Kazinczy Ferenc Általános Iskola és Alapfokú Művészetoktatási Intézmény, Debrecen, Hungary

Állatok Téli Ünnepe
(Animal Winter Feast)

Holdfény látszik a fákon,
a faluban mély az álom
Az állatok vannak csak ébren,
Gyík lapul fűszálon, nyuszi ugrik az erdei ágnak...
Most a Télapóra várnak!

A Robin in the Snow

I saw a robin in the snow
He was moving very slow
He was shivering and alone
He was almost skin and bone

I got him seeds and crumbs from bread
I made him a cosy little bed
He ate and ate and grew and grew
Some time later, he waved and flew.

Golden Star

Twinkling bauble, golden star
I can see you from afar
There's a fairy on the tree
Smiling down at you and me
There's a Christmas pudding
And a Christmas roast
The Christmas cards are in the post
Opening presents for you and me
They are under the Christmas tree

People are snapping Christmas crackers
All the dogs are chewing the wrappers
Santa always has a beer
And all his elves have two big ears
Twinkling bauble, golden star
I can see you from afar.

Állatok Téli Ünnepe *by* Ádám János Fülöp, Európai Iskola, Luxembourg
Golden Star *by* Francesca Morley, Boskenwyn School, Helston, Cornwall, England
A Robin in the Snow *by* Sinéad O'Brien, St Patrick's GNS, Cork

If I Was an Angel

If I was an angel
Way up in the sky
I'd always watch over you
And watch you go by

If I was an angel
Just for a day
I'd send you happiness
And watch you play

I don't need to be an angel
To watch you from above
I can still be your angel
And send you my love.

Champion de Foot
(Football Champion)

Je suis un champion de foot
Je n'aime pas prendre de petites chutes
Je joue au milieu du terrain –
Mais je ne joue pas à la main!
J'adore regarder Arsenal
Mais quand ils perdent ca me fait mal
Mon joueur préféré est Fabregas
C'est vraiment un très grand as.

28
If I Was an Angel *by* Beth Curtayne Gardiner, St Patrick's GNS, Cork
Champion de Foot *by* Thomas Carton, Enfants Francophones de Cork
Angel *by* Aoife Leonard, St Columba's NS, Dring, Co. Longford

The Day the Elephant Came to School

Yesterday an elephant came to school
While the teacher screamed 'Help!' the children seemed cool
The teacher quickly called the zoo
Get him out before he does a poo!
The keeper came with a giant net
'Oh no!' yelled the teacher, 'The carpet's all wet!'
The elephant gave a great loud roar
And stomped his way through to the door
The enormous elephant then made a wave
And to the petrified teacher he gave
A sloppy wet lick upon her head
The poor teacher suddenly went bright red
She just couldn't take anymore
And collapsed straight onto the floor!

The Day the Elephant Came to School *by Sarah Lockhart, Ovens NS, Co. Cork*
Elephant *by Tara Ní Ríogáin, GS an Ghoirt Álainn, Cork*

Az Élet Öröme
(Joy of Life)

Tegnap reggel, amint felébredtem,
A kertembe sietve kimentem.
Lassan ébredezve körbe néztem;
Mellettem egy hangya dolgozott éppen.
Morzsát cipelve elment mellettem,
De visszanézett és integetni kezdett.
Valamit mondott, de nem értettem,
Egy méh zümmögése elnyomott mindent.
Hozzám repült a méh, féltem, hogy megcsíp,
De megnyugtatott, csak mondani akart valamit.
„Én vagyok a legszorgosabb méh a világon.
Az életet éppen ezért imádom.”
Végre a hangyának is jutott beszéd;
Ő azt mondta: „Az élet szép.”
Még a madár is a fán azt csicsergi,
Hogy élni kell és szeretni.a

30 Az Élet Öröme *by* Bálint Bodor, Belová Zrínyi Ilona Általános Iskola, Kecskemét, Hungary
Dolphin *by* Bálint Macsuga, Kesjár Csaba Általános Iskola, Budaörs, Hungary

Teplé Léto Přišlo
(Warm Summer Came)

Léto přišlo
prázdniny začaly
Teplé dny právě počaly

Ovoce zraje
lidé se koupají
Ted' už žádné starosti nemají.

When Summer Came In

I saw the wool
And was afraid
I'd be all tangled up
In that giant pile
Of colourful summer.

Teplé Léto Přišlo *by* Jan Křemenák, Gymnázium Jiřího Ortena, Kutná Hora, Czech Republic
When Summer Came In *by* Eoin Murtagh, Emper NS, Ballynacargy, Co. Westmeath
Under the Ocean *by* Masha Brazhnik, Alexandrovskaya Gymnasia, Sumy, Ukraine

Football Field

Grass grows so slowly
So so so so so slowly
Every long day.

It's Nearly My Birthday

It's nearly my birthday
I'm so excited
Big presents, small present
And a giant birthday cake!
I feel like I'm a billionaire
I just can't wait.

My Dog

When I walk with my dog
Through the park
The creatures will run
Because boy, does he bark!
He tangles my legs
And runs around trees
He sprints so fast
He drags me to my knees
When we get home
He's dirty and wet
But he's a great puppy
And a very good pet.

Football Field *by* Luke Walsh, Lettergesh NS, Co. Galway
32 My Dog *by* Jack Hever, Scoil Mhuire Gan Smál, Ballymote, Co. Sligo
It's Nearly My Birthday *by* Darren Culliney, St Patrick's NS, Ballinamuck, Co. Longford
Me and Sally *by* Genevieve Mohan, Cork School Project

Tree

House builder   Animal shelter
Furniture supplier   Scenery enhancer
Food supplier   Leaf sprouter
Field worker   Wind blocker
Fire fuel   Rain gatherer
Soil compactor
Sun blocker
Air cleaner
Sap storer
Bird nester
Moss collector
House protector.

Tree by Darragh Faherty, Lettergesh NS, Co. Galway
Rooted Trees by Klára Kopčíková, Gymnázium Jiřího Ortena, Kutná Hora, Czech Republic

My Dream Horse

I have a horse
I love him so dear
A black heavy cob
That stays so near
We wander through golden buttercup fields
And splash in the lovely blue sea
My Blaze, my Blaze
Means everything to me!

34 My Dream Horse *by* Caitlín Canavan O'Driscoll, SN Rae na Scríne, Rosscarbery, Co. Cork
Champion *by* Imogen Green, Grange NS, Clonmel, Co. Tipperary

Watching Myself Sing

I love to open my mouth
And hear my voice coming out
The words just come my way
They may not make a song
But I continue to carry on
I listen to myself
And imagine how it could be
For people to see
And listen to me.

Watching Myself Sing by Leanne Courtney, St Dominic's NS, Kenagh, Co. Longford
Les Chanteuses by Naomi Boume, Enfants Francophones de Cork

The Christmas Tree

Oh Christmas tree
So bright with decorations
Light so bright as the sun
Decorations as beautiful as a dress
You are as green as leaves
With presents under your strong trunk
And with a star as shiny as gold
And in Christmas, children come next to you
For them, you are their best decoration
The best as the best car model
Oh Christmas tree you are
The most special Christmas symbol!

The Christmas Tree *by Luke Fenech, Stella Maris College, Ġzira, Malta*
Winter *by Leanne Ní Cheocháin, GS Bheanntraí, Co. Cork*

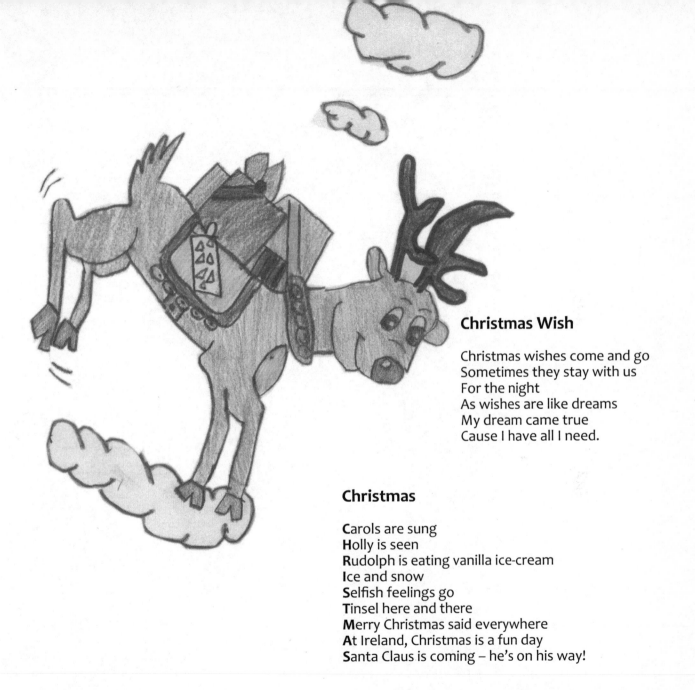

Christmas Wish

Christmas wishes come and go
Sometimes they stay with us
For the night
As wishes are like dreams
My dream came true
Cause I have all I need.

Christmas

Carols are sung
Holly is seen
Rudolph is eating vanilla ice-cream
Ice and snow
Selfish feelings go
Tinsel here and there
Merry Christmas said everywhere
At Ireland, Christmas is a fun day
Santa Claus is coming – he's on his way!

Christmas Wish by Danielle Ní Chonghaile, GS Bheanntraí, Co. Cork
Christmas by Abdullah Ali, Grianach House School, Galway
La Renna Felice by Andrea Cascianelli, Scuola Primaria dell'Istituto Comprensivo 'P. Serafini – L. di Stefano', Sulmona, Italy

Snow

Snow
Cold white
Falls from clouds
I play with snow
White.

Snow *by* Nina Dorogaia, Grianach House School, Galway
Playing in the Snow *by* Sara Jaglikovska, OU Johan Hajnrih Pestaloci, Skopje, Macedonia

School Days

We started school when we were four
Our teachers met us at the door
They gave us a big smile
And we smiled back
And on our backs
A brand new sack

We played games
And had great fun
But in the yard
We could not run
We ate our lunch – yummy!
All healthy food in our tummy

The day was great
We have to say
Can't wait for tomorrow
Another day
Sleep tight till morning comes
And dream of stories, books, sums...

School Days *by* Lauren Kelly, St Patrick's GNS, Cork
My House *by* Cian Laffey, Lettergesh NS, Co. Galway

Neuredna Slova
(Untidy Letters)

Takmičila se neuredna slova
po papiru se razbacala,
plesala, skakutala.

Priča se poremetila,
iz bilježnice izletjela.

Neuredna, razbacana slova
u bilježnici su zaspala.
Svakim danom sve više
razbacanu pjesmu su stvarala.

I Made Humpty Dumpty

I made Humpty Dumpty
And gave him a blue hat
And a red coat, new shoes
And coloured him strong
He sits on a wall all day long
Has a big head and short legs
He falls off the wall
I tell him, 'you're clumsy'
And put him back up again.

Neuredna Slova *by* Anabel Babić, OŠ Poreč, Croatia
I Made Humpty Dumpty *by* Conor Clancy, Stonepark NS, Co. Longford
Drawing *by* Aurora del Signore, Scuola Primaria dell'Istituto Comprensivo 'P. Serafini – L. di Stefano', Sulmona, Italy

41

Lulet
(Flowers)

Dola për shëtitje me prindërit e mi
Në parqet e livadhet e këtij qyteti
U gëzova shumë nga ajo që pashë
Cicërima zogjshmë ndiqnin plot gaz
U ulja dhe vazhdova t'i soditja me admirim
Thashë; 'Të marr ca lule për vëllanë tim'.

Jaro Je Ráj
(Spring is Paradise)

Květiny voní;
vrací se slunce,
v potoce vidíme
krásného sumce

Ptáci si zpívají
čistý je vzduch
na lukách slyšíme
bzučení much

Cítíme svěžest
příjemný je kraj
jaro je prostě
jaro je ráj!

42 Lulet *by* Euxhen Hasanaj, Shkolla Kongresi i Lushnjës, Tirana, Albania
Jaro Je Ráj *by* Eliška Holubová, Gymnázium Jiřího Ortena, Kutná Hora, Czech Republic
Wanda the Busy Bee *by* Michaela Broe, St Patrick's GNS, Cork

Mise Ar Mo Rothar

Mise ar mo rothar
É daite gorm is bán
Mise ar mo rothar
Is mé ag dul le fán

Mise ar mo rothar
Ní fhaca mé an poll
Mise de mo rothar
Is mé ag siúl go mall.

Mise Ar Mo Rothar by Meadhbh O'Callaghan, GS an Ghoirt Álainn, Cork
My Bike by Bruno di Benedetto, Scuola Primaria dell'Istituto Comprensivo 'P. Serafini – L. di Stefano', Sulmona, Italy

Le Vent
(The Wind)

Le vent, le vent comme il souffle tout le temps,
Le vent, le vent j'aime comme il est bruyant,
Il me cajole et me fait tourner,
Mes cheveux s'envolent et je frisonne!

Le vent, le vent tu peux être un grand danger,
Le vent, le vent j'ai vu le bateau chavirer,
Mais moi j'aime t'écouter.

Le Vent (poem and drawing) *by Sophie Tuffy, Enfants Francophones de Cork*

When I Opened a Snowflake

I was a lonely person
Who had no money
When a special snowflake
Landed on my nose
I opened the snowflake
And discovered contentment
Saw in a window
People putting up Christmas
Children excited for Santa
The smell of cookies
Oh yum, yum, yum
Out of that snowflake
My life changed forever.

December 24

Egyszer voltam egy erdőben,
hoztam meleget egy kendőben
'Esik a hó, jaj de jó!' – mondtam,
s leszánkóztam

Amikor leértem, a fán egy madár,
a házban naptár
'December 24.' – olvastam,
és tovább szánkóztam

Otthon azt kiabáltam:
'Jaj, de jó volt a hóban!'
S már a karácsonyfa alatt állottam...

Jaj de szép a Karácsony!
Karácsonyi asztal, fenyő, szép ajándék!
Az állatok is ünnepelnek:
ez kész ajándék!

Jaj de szép a Karácsony!
Égnek a gyertyák, sül a kalácsom...

When I Opened a Snowflake *by* Susan Farrelly, St Dominic's NS, Kenagh, Co. Longford
December 24 *by* Ádám János Fülöp, Európai Iskola, Luxembourg

Eyes

I wake up in the morning
In my bed I'm curled
I open up my eyes
My window on the world

I gaze around the room
My lids reluctantly unfurled
I open up my eyes
My window on the world.

Un Mic Palat
(A Small Palace)

Pe o frunză mai pitică,
A căzut una mai mică
Şi-au căzut aşa, pe rând,
Un micuţ palat formând
Furnicile s-au gândit
Că e bun de locuit
Au intrat şi s-au jucat
Şi chiar un nume i-au dat:
,,Palatul furnicăresc",
Cum pe strada Florilor,
,,Palatul Copiilor".

46
Eyes *by* Jack Laffey, Lettergesh NS, Co. Galway
Un Mic Palat *by* Raluca Pop, Şcoala Generală Nr. 4 Bistriţa, Romania
The Painter *by* János Nagyhaju, Fiumei Úti Általános Iskola, Szolnok, Hungary

Argentina

Mi país Argentina
está en la madre americana
En mi país hay maravillas,
muchas, aquí y allá
como La Patagonia, el Culla,
los glaciares, las Tres Cascadas,
el hermoso Valle de las Hadas
y el mar con sus puentes
y sus ríos con sus corrientes
en las que tomamos unos mates.

In the View of a Lifetime

As I stand on a hill
In the view of a lifetime
Overlooking the yellow sand
Blowing in the wind
And the pyramids like wardens
Guard the beams of the sun
Dancing in a yellow paradise

Taking one more look
I see the blue sky hitting
With the yellow on the horizon
Taking in this magical view
Is all I need to know.

Argentina *by* Santiago Esco & Felipe Bonadeo, Sunflower School, Buenos Aires, Argentina
In the View of a Lifetime *by* Mark Thompson, St Mel's NS, Ardagh, Co. Longford
Sipping Mate *by* Santiago Esco and Felipe Bonadeo, Sunflower School, Buenos Aires, Argentina

Dares

Darragh and I are in the park
He dares me
I dare him
Jump up jump down
Off the swing
On the see-saw
No you can't
Yes I can
I wait and see
I jump
I fall
I hurt my knee
I cry out loud
Good gracious me!

Jumping Foot

Ticklish foot jumps shockingly
In a chocolate swimming pool
Because a slithery snake bit
Off its big toe quite sneakily.

Dares *by* Darragh O'Shea, Scoil Mhuire NS, Schull, Co. Cork
Jumping Foot *by* Cathal Glynn, Lettergesh NS, Co. Galway
Europe *by* Glenn Sheedy, GS an Ghoirt Álainn, Cork

Mare e Cielo
(Sea and Sky)

Il limpido mare all'orizzonte
Col cielo si confonde
Sugli scogli riposano i gabbiani
Sognando paesi lontani
Barche di pescatori in lontananza...
Il mio cuore è colmo di speranza!

My Fish

Like two airplanes,
An orange flash darting, undercover
Catching the light off their gills
Fins waving up and down
Like a soundless chant
Silver eyes keep an unwavering gaze
Bubbling
A toothless grin.

Mare e Cielo *by* Valentina Centofanti, Scuola Primaria dell'Istituto Comprensivo 'P. Serafini – L. di Stefano', Sulmona, Italy
My Fish *by* Foster Piotrow, Jackson Grammar School, New Hampshire, USA
On the Royal Canal *by* Aidan Murtagh, Emper NS, Ballynacargy, Co. Westmeath

Differences

Skies aren't always blue
Deserts aren't always sandy
We aren't all the same.

Differences *by* Andrea Faherty, Lettergesh NS, Co. Galway
Bubble Gum *by* Birte Kirch, Musikschule der Hansestadt Wismar, Germany

I'm an Agent

Oh my gosh, I haven't a clue
What is this thing I have to do
I can't find that lad
That is very bad
I mean one that's driving me mad

In the time since he said that long speech
I've one thousand bandits on a beach
I've arrested a man who hit me
with his giant finger nail
To get away from me to him was a great big fail

'Hey you, over there, do you think you
Would like to see our secret HQ?
Be an Ireland Spying Agent Dude
We've got a gadget that makes cars and food!'

This is what he said to me
But nothing about an entry fee

'See our 10 Most Wanted list
And see if there is one we've missed
Oh, this teleporter phone is the best
It takes you round the world in a minute – no, less!'

He told me this as well as that
And I was scratched in the leg by the HQ cat

'We have a jet pack that makes you fly
A gun that makes you sleep, not die
And if you see a wanted man
You can trap him in a giant can'

This made me really impressed
And guess what: I passed the test!
Hey, what's that? The Wanted Man!
Let's hope this goes to plan…

There, got him!
He's a Scots man with a clan
There, got him!
Trapped him in a giant can!

My Mum Told Me Today

My Mum told me today
The story about the greyhound
About when he retired
He was served a glass of wine
And listened to the radio
He was given the best straw bed
And didn't bother with an alarm
And when he had his girlfriend over
Was served with a delicious meal.

My Mum Told Me Today *by* Áine Byrne, Emper NS, Ballynacargy, Co. Westmeath
Playing by Hanna Dorina Peresztegi, Gyermekkuckó Óvoda, Budapest, Hungary

Podzim
(Autumn)

Už to tady zase máme
podzim jak ho všichni známe
Děti jdou zas do školy
doma budou psát úkoly
Potom už všichni vědí
že budou draka pouštět k nebi
Večer však přijde brzy
a to nás všechny hrozně mrzí
Jednu naději však všichni máme
že Ježíška se brzy dočkáme

Podzim *by* Jakub Rejfek, Gymnázium Jiřího Ortena, Kutná Hora, Czech Republic
Bridge *by* Gerda Seidelmann, Musikschule der Hansestadt Wismar, Germany

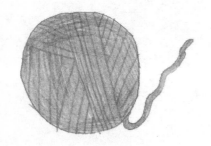

Codladh

Bíonn codladh agam gach oíche
Tar éis gach lae
Dúnaim mo shúile
Is sínim siar go réidh

Má théim a chodladh déanach
Ní bhím ábalta don lá
Caithfidh mé síneadh siar
Chun néal a dhéanamh

Ní féidir ealú uaidh
Is ait an rud é
Tagann sé i gconaí
Codladh, codladh, codladh.

Codladh *by* Ruaidhrí Ó Beaglaoich, Scoil Mhaolchéadair, Muiríoch, Tralee, Co. Kerry
Fat Cat Pat *by* Laura Kerins, Scoil Mhuire gan Smál, Ballymote, Co. Sligo

Barack Obama

Barack Obama is my favourite person in the world
He inspired people with just three words
'Yes We Can' is helpful to me
Because now I can see
What my future will be.

Barack Obama *by* Alison Ní Chonaill, GS Bheanntraí, Co. Cork
Heart of Gold *by* Federica Torti, Scuola Primaria dell'Istituto Comprensivo 'P. Serafini – L. di Stefano', Sulmona, Italy

Az Álom
(The Dream)

Boldogan szárnyalnék, mint a madár,
Tavak, folyók mentén hosszasan,
Mint a Télapó szakáll
De ez sajna mind csak álom,
Ha majd felébredek biztos nagyon bánom

Immár vége a repkedésnek,
Belegondolok, s mégis heherészek
Mert éjjel visszatérek,
És szállok tovább a csillagos égen.

Toamna
(Autumn)

Toamnă rece…
Grea, dar trece…
Noaptea frig,
Ziua soare
Şi mi-e frig, deşi e soare,
Din frunziş cade culoare,
Toamna trece…

Az Álom *by* Lívia Ondrik, Török Ignác Gimnázium, Gödöllő, Hungary
Toamna *by* Alexandra Micu, Şcoala Generală Nr. 4 Bistriţa, Romania
Freedom *by* Tala Salloum, Al Falouja Intermediate School, Alyarmouk Camp, Damascus, Syria

Equality

Some people are professors
And some are protesters
But inside
We are all the same

Girls, boys, cats and dogs
Microsoft and Apple
Everybody can do the same
Some may be stronger
And some weaker
But it all equals
The same.

Equality *by* Aidan Molloy, GS an Ghoirt Álainn, Cork
Albanian Dancer *by* Klodiana Kucana, Shkolla Kongresi i Lushnjës, Tirana, Albania
Irish Dancer *by* Daniel Mooney, GS Uilleog de Burca, Claremorris, Co. Mayo

The Night Sky

When I look at the night sky
I feel I'm looking at a whole new world
The stars are shining brightly
And the moon gives soft beams of light
They greet me so humbly

When I look at the night sky
I don't have a care in the world
The moon shines its beams as proud as a peacock
And the stars shine as grateful as swans

When I look at the night sky
It looks as clear as a crystal
I feel peaceful when I
Look at the night sky.

A Day by the Sea

Mountains so high
Birds in the sky
What a beautiful scene to see

The ocean is blue
The dolphins are too
What a beautiful scene to see

The sun is setting
Time to go home
What a beautiful day had we.

Red Riding Hood Remembers

Jack running up a hill
And getting some water
Going home and making
Himself a cup of tea.

A Day by the Sea by Sophie Murray, St Patrick's GNS, Cork
Red Riding Hood Remembers by Emma McCord, Stonepark NS, Co. Longford
Ballet Dancer by Hannah Ní Mhuirneáin, GS Bheanntraí, Co. Cork
Buachaill by Bréanainn Ó Bruic, Scoil Mhaolchéadair, Muiríoch, Tralee, Co. Kerry

Magically Suspended

All the colour in the world
Like the rainbow holding my hair
Magically suspended right up in the air
Even living in our faces

All the colour in the world
All the stars curled and swirled
Like the world gets fuller and fuller
Yes, I think everyone loves colour.

Magically Suspended *by* Sinéad Bannon, St Mel's NS, Ardagh, Co. Longford
City Silhouette *by* Kristýna Nýrttora, Gymnázium Jiřího Ortena, Kutná Hora, Czech Republic

Flowers

Flowers, flowers
So pretty, so beautiful
Spring brings daffodils
Bright yellow, so original
It also brings blossoms
Roses, too
They bring such greatness
To the season

Summer brings daisy
Fun so enjoyable
Lights up the season
With its white petals

Last is winter
Last season of the year
With its snowy snowdrop
Snowy white cheer

Flowers, flowers
How I love you!
Shining the year
With your beautiful colours.

Flowers *by* Brendan Whitehead, Scoil Mhuire Gan Smál, Ballymote, Co. Sligo
My Back Garden by Aoife Keating, Grange NS, Clonmel, Co. Tipperary **61**

Во Новиот Милениум
(In the New Millennium)

Сообраќајот е густ
во нашиот град.
во воздухот има
многу, многу чад

За да имаме
воздух
чист и свеж,
велосипед
да возиме
и да одиме пеш

Сакам да има
коли со педали,
кој ќе ги смисли
ќе добие медали!

Тогаш почист ќе биде
целиот свет
и повеќе ќе има
пеперутки в лет!

62 Во Новиот Милениум *by* Veronika Poposka, OU Johan Hajnrih Pestaloci, Skopje, Macedonia
(Opposite) Let's Celebrate Spring *by* Sara Jaglikovska, OU Johan Hajnrih Pestaloci, Skopje, Macedonia

LET'S CELEBRATE SPRING

A Horseman Enters a Town at Night

The black darkness turns pink
It's time for the horseman to arrive
The brave warrior has waited so long
He jumps on his velvet painted horse

The town is still, nothing to hear
The pink sky is now breathing grey
The horseman looks around
The remains of nothing and everything

He touches the sky and it turns
Soft blue with flocks of birds
He touches the fields and trees
And blends the earth with red

God gets back on his horse
And returns to heaven.

A Horseman Enters a Town at Night *by* Róisín Costello, Ballyleague NS, Co. Roscommon
Horse *by* Jacqueline Marková, St Patrick's GNS, Cork

There Wasn't Space

When I drew the crib
I made Jesus too small
And the star too big
There wasn't space
To put the tree in
There wasn't space
For the cow, lamb and horse
There wasn't space
To put the Three Wise Men in
There wasn't space
To put the shepherds in
There just wasn't space!

There Wasn't Space *by* Ben Victory, St Mel's NS, Ardagh, Co. Longford
Horse *by* Clodagh Linehan, St Patrick's GNS, Cork

My Fairy Friends

Please do not tell anyone
There's a secret I've got to tell
Pinky promise with your finger
And cross your heart as well

I've fairies in my garden!
Magical, crazy and fun
Scientists might want to study them
So you can't tell anyone!

I play with them every evening
Before I go to bed
My parents think I'm brushing my teeth
But I'm learning some magic instead

They taught me how to turn my supper
Into sugary tasty sweets
They even taught me in my lessons
A hundred ways to cheat

But for some peculiar reason
The morning after we play
I never can remember
Coming up to bed to lay

Maybe when we're in the yard
I suddenly fall asleep
And they magically lift me up to bed
Without making a peep

Do you want to come to my house tonight
To see my fairy crew?
I just hope that they are strong enough
To lift you up to bed too.

I Just Choose Blue

I don't know why I choose blue
Maybe because it's white today
Maybe because it's meant to be
Blue the colour in the ocean
Swiftly flowing to its end
The colour in my eye.

68 I Just Choose Blue *by* Aisling Carroll, St Mel's NS, Ardagh, Co. Longford
Meeting Prince Charming *by* Victoria Kingston, Scoil Mhuire Junior School, Cork

Farming With My Dad

My Dad works hard on the farm
He brings the cows from the Fort field for milking
He'd never plough that, he says it's unlucky
I think of people cooking over open fires
Children playing pitch and toss
As I feed the calves with Dad.

Farming With My Dad by Liam Ronan, SN Rae na Scríne, Rosscarbery, Co. Cork
Scarecrow by Niamh Quinn, Scoil Mhuire gan Smál, Ballymote, Co. Sligo

Dream World

The beautiful scenery
The aromatic scents
Children running and racing
The wind blowing against me
The fresh sea air
Away in my own little world.

I Dropped a Thought

I dropped a thought in a wishing well
I missed it all day
The thought grew bigger and bigger
Like a drop in the ocean
Thinking of a world that never ends
Oh! What a thought I'd dropped
In that wishing well.

Dream World by Cathal Mullins, Ovens NS, Co. Cork
I Dropped a Thought by Lisa Keegan, St Mel's NS, Ardagh, Co. Longford
Pirate Ship by Jack Mahony, Scoil Phádraig Naofa, Bandon, Co. Cork

Lollipops

Lollipops, lollipops
Aren't they sweet
Small and tasty
So petite!

Apple, strawberry
Lemon and lime
Me and Chloe eat them
All the time

Lollipops taste like
Heaven on earth
They even taste better
Than dessert

Lollipops, lollipops
Yum yum yum
They remind me of
A little hum
Which goes a little
Bit like this –

Lollipops, lollipops
Ooh, lolli, lolli, lolli, lolli
Lollipops!
Aaahh…
Yum yum yum yum.

Lollipops by Eimer Conlon, Scoil Mhuire Gan Smál, Ballymote, Co. Sligo
Teddy Bear by Lisa McGrath, Scoil Mhuire gan Smál, Ballymote, Co. Sligo

Internet

Intelligent
Net
Teaching
Exploring
Resource
Need
Enormous
Telephone

Internet *By* Dominik Husar, OŠ Josipovac, Croatia
Spider, Spider *by* Helena Schindler, Musikschule der Hansestadt Wismar, Germany

You Say

You say I can't win the race
I say I can so, in your face
You say I can't read the book
I say I can so, take a look
You say I can't make the cake
I say I can so, watch me bake
You say I can't climb the wall
I say I can, I'll prove it all!

I Always Look Forward

I always look forward
To a Friday afternoon
When my brother James
Collects me from school
I'll never forget
On the 19th of November last
He parked on the other side of the road
I felt stranded like a princess
In a pile of muck outside the school gate
He ran across the road
Picked me up and put me on his shoulders
And carried me to the car
He put me in and made sure
I had my seatbelt on.

You Say *by* Ellen Horgan, GS an Ghoirt Álainn, Cork
I Always Look Forward *by* Mary Rogers, St Columba's NS, Dring, Co. Longford
I Want to Live in a Lovely Family *by* Denis Ivanov, Smorgon Educational Centre for Children and Youth, Belarus

Animal Familier
(Family Pet)

Mon chien Rasta
N'aime pas les chats
Il est doux comme tout
Aussi doux que mon doudou
Tous les soirs mon papa le sort
A l'heure où moi je dors!
Il a changé ma vie
J'en suis vraiment ravie!

74 Animal Familier *by* Louise Hennessy, Enfants Francophones de Cork
The Chain is the Price of Loyalty *by* Réka Komjáthy,
Ilosvai Selymes Péter Általános Iskola és Alapfokú Művészetoktatási Intézmény, Abaújszántó, Hungary

I Used to Love Watching Ronaldo

Speeding past defenders
Getting lots of goals
With an ocean of skill

When I watched Ronaldo
I could hear the crowd shout
GOAL – GOAL – GOAL!

When he left United
I was really mad
For ninety million grand
We needed a new star
For the theatre of our dreams

Dani, Hernández, Scholes, Giggs?
No, it had to be Rooney
Rooney can win the League
We don't need you, Ronaldo
Oh, let him to Madrid!
We don't need you, Ronaldo.

I Used to Love Watching Ronaldo *by* Paul Farley, St Colmcille's NS, Aughnacliffe, Co. Longford
Goalie *by* Niamh McGee, Scoil Mhuire gan Smál, Ballymote, Co. Sligo

Shooting Stars

A shooting star show
Makes the sky glow
Lie on the grass
Watch them whizz past
Night by night
Day by day
Shooting stars come
But quickly fade away.

76 Shooting Stars *by* Sinéad Buckley, Scoil Mhuire Junior School, Cork
Asteroid *by* James Quinn, St Mel's NS, Ardagh, Co. Longford

Staring Heavenwards

As Jupiter loops below the moon
I stare at everything going on up there
And feel the creak in my neck
Straining for so long
I never felt the minutes ticking away
So far out there in space.

Staring Heavenwards by Fergal Farrell, St Mel's NS, Ardagh, Co. Longford
NASA Rocket by Johnny Finnan, St Mel's NS, Ardagh, Co. Longford

My Family

My Dad is hilarious and he is so fun
My Mum is helpful and she likes to bake buns
My brother is so clever and he is so tall
But my sister is amazing and she is so small
My brother is so mean and he is so rough
But me, oh me, I am such a pup.

My Family *by* Úna Ní Luinneacháin, GS Bheanntraí, Co. Cork
Chubby Mummy *by* Caroline O'Connor, St Patrick's GNS, Cork

Il Fruscio del Mare
(The Whisper of the Sea)

Il fruscio del mare
Che muove le onde
È un incantesimo dolce
Del mare che sta sussurrando.

Il Fruscio del Mare *by* Francesca Fabbri, Scuola Primaria dell'Istituto Comprensivo 'P. Serafini – L. di Stefano', Sulmona, Italy
Surf Shop *by* Patrick Finan, Scoil Mhuire gan Smál, Ballymote, Co. Sligo

Der Willi mit dem Motorroller
(Willi with the Motorbike)

Dem Willi weht der Wind um die Ohren,
doch die Jess ist schon fast erfroren!
Dem Willi geht es gut,
wenn er mit seiner Hupe tut.

Die beiden fahren mit dem Motorroller
Und kriegen dabei gewiss keinen Hitzekoller.
Doch Jess ist stark wie Pfefferfisch,
und ihre Liebe ist noch frisch,
denn sie traf ihn kurz vor einer Stund,
beim Gassigehen mit ihrem Hund!

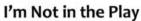

I'm Not in the Play

I'm not in the play
Couldn't go, too busy on the farm
Looking after all the animals
In the stable for the Christmas play
I have to feed the hens and ducks
And bring the donkey and cows
Some hay
I love feeding them.

80 Der Willi mit dem Motorroller *by* Luisa Bergholz, Musikschule der Hansestadt Wismar, Germany
I'm Not in the Play *by* Thomas Mooney, St Columba's NS, Dring, Co. Longford
Watering the Flowers *by* Dávid Wéber, D-B-M Mikrotérségi Általános Iskola, Gimnázium és Szakiskola, Madocsa, Hungary

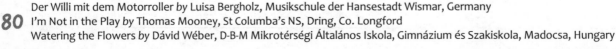

Dogs Rock

I love dogs –
I have fourteen and seven pups –
It's hard work
Playing with all of them

It can be tiring
Sometimes they bite
But it's hard not to forgive
They're all so cute
My mother doesn't allow them
In the house

But still I play with them outside
They're all different breeds
I have no favourites
They're just all so cute to me.

Dogs Rock *by* Sarah Farrelly, St Colmcille's NS, Aughnacliffe, Co. Longford
Animal Band *by* Leanne Kidney, Presentation Primary School, Bandon, Co. Cork

Fellow Frost

He killed my potato
He's a danger to crops
He destroys the plant
And rots the top

He killed my potato
He's not very nice
He scares poor foxes
And blows away mice

On cold mornings
On cold nights
He hides in the grass
And turns off your lights

Winter's his mountain
Where babies have cried
Fellow frost, run
Fellow frost, hide.

The Misery Man

A man came to my house
Just the other day
I don't know how he did it
But he took the fun away

It's like he just stepped inside
And turned the world upside down
Now on everyone's face
There's a miserable frown

The man that came looked like an ordinary man
Except he was holding a sack
He walked through the door just like a ghost
And turned everything grey and black

He took the fun, he took the games
And put them in his sack
All I do now all day
Is pray that he won't be back

This man was very tall
And also very slim
I wish I knew what he did to me
So I could do it to him.

82 Fellow Frost *by* Simon O'Neill, St Patrick's NS, Ballinamuck, Co. Longford
The Misery Man *by* Eiman Ilyas, Grianach House School, Galway

Over the Wall

Over the wall
The words debate
Why in this country
There's so much hate
Recession, recession
Please disappear
You are far too near
Go away, I don't want
You to be near.

Over the Wall *by* Aimée Higgins, Emper NS, Ballynacargy, Co. Westmeath
Angel versus Demon *by* Claudia Mazzone, Fiumei Úti Általános Iskola, Szolnok, Hungary

Ronaldo and Rooney

Ronaldo and Rooney
Sitting in a tree
K-i-c-k-i-n-g
First come kicks
Then come goals
They keep playing
Till they lose their souls.

Ronaldo and Rooney *by* Mohammad Ilyas, Grianach House School, Galway
Free Kick *by* Cian O'Brien, Ballyleague NS, Co. Roscommon

Lego

Lego, Lego, Lego
the world of creativity and fun
I like building houses and towns
filled with Lego hounds
And great big skyscrapers
with big red signs on top
Oh how could you survive
if you didn't have Lego?

Lego by Karla Bester, Scoil Barra Naofa, Monkstown, Co. Cork
Sunshine City by Grigore Chis, Şcoala Generală Nr. 4 Bistriţa, Romania

Sándor Petőfi and the Griffin by Ádám Wéber, D-B-M Mikrotérségi Általános Iskola, Gimnázium és Szakiskola, Madocsa, Hungary